LIVING IN LOVE AND FAITH

A CONCISE INTRODUCTION AND REVIEW

MARTIN DAVIE

The Latimer Trust

ISBN 978-1-906327-69-9

Published by the Latimer Trust March 2021.

The Latimer Trust (formerly Latimer House, Oxford) is a conservative Evangelical research organisation within the Church of England, whose main aim is to promote the history and theology of Anglicanism as understood by those in the Reformed tradition. Interested readers are welcome to consult its website for further details of its many activities.

The Latimer Trust

London N14 4PS UK

Registered Charity: 1084337

Company Number: 4104465

Web: www.latimertrust.org

E-mail: administrator@latimertrust.org

CONTENTS

1. What is the background to Living in Love and Faith?

The immediate background to Living in Love and Faith (LLF) was the decision by the Church of England's General Synod in February 2017 not to 'take note' (in other words, give approval to) the House of Bishops' report 'Marriage and Same-Sex Relationships after the Shared Conversations'.[1]

In response to this vote, the Archbishops of Canterbury and York wrote an open letter in which they said, among other things, that the House of Bishops would produce 'a large-scale teaching document around the subject of human sexuality'.[2]

The LLF material – a suite of resources for 'Christian teaching and learning about identity, sexuality, relationships and marriage' – is the fulfilment of that promise.[3]

2. How was LLF produced?

LLF was produced by a large team of forty-nine invited participants. These participants were male and female, lay and ordained, they had a range of expertise, and they held a range of different views on the matters under discussion.[4] They worked in four groups covering the Bible, doctrine and ethics, history, and science – and each group was chaired by a diocesan bishop. The work of these groups was overseen by a co-ordinating group

---

[1] On the vote not to 'take note', see http://www.bbc.co.uk/news/uk-38982013 and https://uk.reuters.com/article/uk-religion-britain-anglicans/church-of-england-stance-on-gay-marriage-in-disarray-after-vote-idUKKBN15U2L9. Church of England, 'Marriage and Same Sex Relationships after the Shared Conversations: A Report from the House of Bishops', GS 2055, November 2016, www.churchofengland.org

[2] https://www.churchofengland.org/sites/default/files/2017-11/abc-and-aby-joint-letter.pdf

[3] Church of England, *Living in Love and Faith: Christian teaching and learning about identity, sexuality, relationships and marriage* (London: Church House Publishing, 2020). Available as a pdf from https://www.churchofengland.org/resources/living-love-and-faith

[4] The list of participants can be found at 'Living in Love and Faith group members' at https://www.churchofengland.org/resources/living-love-and-faith/living-love-and-faith-group-members.

of bishops and consultants. The LLF process was chaired by the Bishop of Coventry, Christopher Cocksworth, and its day-to-day running was overseen by the 'enabling officer', Dr Eeva John.

3. What materials does the LLF 'suite of resources' contain?

The LLF 'suite of resources' contains five types of material:

- A 480-page book (this is the central and most important resource).

- 16 podcasts consisting of edited conversations between people who were part of the LLF process.

- 17 films in which individuals, couples and families describe their own experiences of the matters being discussed by LLF.

- A 5-session study course, available online or as a printed booklet, which looks at: what it means to learn together as followers of Jesus Christ; how our identity in Christ relates to sex and gender; the kind of relationships to which God calls us; where our bodies and sex fit into all of this; and how diversity and difference affect out life together as a church.

- An online library of 323 additional resources, containing both background papers produced for the LLF process and details of books and papers published elsewhere.

4. What is the purpose of the LLF material?

The purpose of the LLF material is explained by the bishops in the 'Invitation' at the start of the LLF book and in the 'Appeal' at the end.

In the 'Invitation' they write that the book has come about because:

> there is disagreement within the people of God, including among us, the Bishops of the Church of England. There are disagreements about same-sex relationships and the Christian understanding of marriage as the Church of England has received it. There are also disagreements about pastoral practice in relation to gender identity, sexuality and

relationships more generally. The roots of these disagreements relate to Scripture, doctrine, ethics and the nature of the Church, including the Church of England.[5]

In the 'Appeal', they write that, in face of these differences:

It remains clear that all of us – bishops included – need to go on learning from each other and from all who seek the way of truth. That is the purpose of the Living in Love and Faith learning resources – to help us to learn and discern together so that right judgements and godly decisions can be made about our common life.[6]

5. What will happen now that LLF has been published?

According to the statement about LLF issued by the Church of England on 9 November 2020[7], three things will now happen:

First, a period of 'church-wide learning and engagement' will take place during 2021. What this will mean in practice in the light in the face of the continuing coronavirus pandemic is not yet clear.

Secondly, parallel to this, 'A group of bishops, chaired by the Bishop of London, Sarah Mullally, the "Next Steps Group," will lead a process of discernment and decision-making about a way forward for the church in relation to human identity, sexuality, relationships and marriage.'

Thirdly, the House of Bishops will bring 'the discernment and decision-making to a timely conclusion in 2022' and the bishops will then bring a proposal for the way forward for the Church of England to the General Synod.

---

[5] *Living in Love and Faith*, p. 3.
[6] *Living in Love and Faith*, p. 422.
[7] The Church of England, 'Living in Love and Faith resources published as bishops issue appeal to Church to "listen and learn together"' at https://www.churchofengland.org/news-and-media/news-and-statements/living-love-and-faith-resources-published-bishops-issue-appeal.

6. What is in the LLF book?

Foreword

The LLF book begins with a Foreword by the Archbishops of Canterbury and York. In this Foreword, they explain that that in the LLF material:

> We seek to understand the mind of God revealed in Scripture, our final authority in which we find all things necessary for salvation. We listen to the Church present and past and universal. We use our reason and understanding, drawing on the best thinking of the natural and human sciences. In that process of threefold listening we commit to learning, from God and through each other, in the spirit and light of that perfect love.[8]

An Invitation

Following the Foreword, there is an 'Invitation' from the Bishops of the Church of England in which they refer to the account of the feeding of the five thousand in John 6 and explain that the LLF book and accompanying resources are an invitation to those in the Church of England to be likewise nourished by Christ:

> the book and its accompanying resources invite us all to sit down together with each other, and, like the crowds, to be nourished by Christ. It is an invitation made in faith: that God will provide the nourishment that we need to better understand God's purposes in relation to human identity, sexuality, relationships and marriage. It is an invitation that carries with it the power of God's love: the love of the one who created us and cares for us in the seemingly impossible dilemmas we face as a church with regard to our different perspectives on these matters.[9]

They go on to say that the purpose of the LLF book is to try to:

---

[8] *Living in Love and Faith*, p. vii.
[9] *Living in Love and Faith*, p. 2.

create a space for us all to rediscover the compassionate, self-giving and abundant love of Christ in and among us as we learn together. It is about being led deeper into the truth about the God we encounter in Scripture: the God who has spoken in love to our broken world in the life, death and resurrection of Jesus; the God who, in renewing all things (Matthew 19.28), is calling us to the hope in which we were saved, a hope for what we do not yet see, but wait for with patience. It is about proclaiming the kingdom of God and making Christ known in the world he came by grace to save and bring to fulness of life.[10]

The structure of the main part of the book
The main part of the book is divided into five parts:

- Part One – Reflecting: what have we received?

- Part Two – Paying attention: what is going on?

- Part Three – Making Connections: where are we in God's story?

- Part Four – Seeking answers: how do we hear God?

- Part Five – Conversing: What can we learn from each other?

At the end of each part there are a series of what are called 'Encounters' – brief snapshots of the lives of twenty individuals and congregations from across the Church of England who shared their experiences with the LLF group.

Part One – Reflecting: what have we received?
The purpose of this part (Chapters 1–4): 'is to set our questions about human identity, sexuality, relationships and marriage in the context of God's gift of life'.[11]

Chapter 1: The gift of life 'invites us to wonder at the gift of abundant, eternal life that is offered to us through the redemptive life, death and resurrection of Jesus Christ'.[12]

---

[10] *Living in Love and Faith*, p. 6.
[11] *Living in Love and Faith*, p. 10.
[12] *Living in Love and Faith*, p. 10.

Chapter 2: The gift of life in relationship 'shows us that this gift of life is a gift of relationship. It explores some of the characteristics of our relationships that flow from God's gift of life, a gift renewed through the reconciling work of Jesus Christ and made known in the community of love formed around him'.[13]

Chapter 3: The gift of marriage 'explains the biblical and historical roots of the church's understanding of marriage as a lifelong, faithful relationship between one man and one woman'.[14]

Chapter 4: The gift of learning draws Part One to an end with an explanation of:

> how, in the rest of the book, we will go about learning together – being taught together by Christ – about human identity, sexuality, relationships and marriage. It explains the rationale for engaging with the Bible, the church's tradition, history and the sciences in the search for truth. It explores how and why we also need to be good observers of the world in which God has placed us, and of the lived experiences which call us to understand God's presence in human experience.[15]

Part Two – Paying attention: what is going on?
The purpose of this part (Chapters 5–7):

> is to take a careful look at what is happening in the world around us with regard to identity, sexuality, relationships and marriage. We describe, as dispassionately as possible, what is going on in God's world with its mix of goodness and fallenness, of glory and human weakness.[16]

Chapter 5: Society looks at contemporary British society. The chapter is in three sections:

---

[13] *Living in Love and Faith*, p. 10.
[14] *Living in Love and Faith*, p. 10.
[15] *Living in Love and Faith*, p. 10.
[16] *Living in Love and Faith*, p. 60.

- The first section is about the changing patterns of relationships. It looks in turn at singleness, marriage, procreation and the well-being of children, friendship, and loneliness.

- The second section is about sexual activity. It looks in turn at sex and fulfilment, the commodification of sex, freedom and consent, pornography, domestic abuse and child sexual abuse.

- The third section is about identity and self-understanding. It looks in turn at sexual orientation, gender identity and the relationship between gender and sex.

Chapter 6: Science looks at what science tells us about issues of sex and gender. The chapter begins by exploring the complexity and difficulty surrounding the scientific study of sexuality and gender. It then looks at what we can learn from science about sexual orientation, gender identity and intersex. The final part of the chapter then considers what science has to teach us about sex and well-being, sexual orientation and gender identity as medical diagnoses, the relationship between the mental health of LGBT people and social stigma, efforts to change people's sexual orientation and gender identity, and the nature of gender transition procedures.

Chapter 7: Religion looks at developments with regard to LGBTI+ issues in the Jewish, Sikh, Hindu and Muslim communities, the Church of England and the Anglican Communion.

Part Three – Making Connections: where are we in God's story?
The purpose of this part (Chapters 8–12) 'is to explore current Christian thinking and discussions about human identity, sexuality, and marriage.'[17]

Chapter 8: A story of love and faith with hope begins by explaining that 'love is the reason for creation; and sharing love with God is the reason for the creation of human beings.'[18] It then explores the relationship between love, faith and hope.

---

[17] *Living in Love and Faith*, p. 164.
[18] *Living in Love and Faith*, p. 171.

Chapter 9: A story that embraces all life explores what the Bible has to say about the theological significance of the human body, relationships, family life, and the relationship between sex and power.

Chapter 10: A story about being human looks at what the Christian faith has to say about human dignity, human diversity, human identity and human sinfulness. The chapter notes that the church's disagreements about gender and sexuality are:

> disagreements about whether certain aspects of human experience, in the areas of gender and sexuality, are to be viewed as reflecting the goodness and God-given diversity of humans as created in God's image, or as marks of the brokenness of that created image which God is working to restore.[19]

Chapter 11: A story about being Church considers the three topics of the holiness of the Church, inclusion and exclusion, and the relationship between disagreement and communion. The chapter notes that there is disagreement about how significant disagreements about sexuality, gender identity, relationships and marriage are for the life of the Church. It also notes that the key question in discussion of these issues is which patterns of life are consistent, and which inconsistent, with the holiness of God which the life of the Church is called to reflect.

Chapter 12: A story about ways of human loving begins by looking at how holy living necessarily involves self-denial or self-discipline. It then looks at celibacy and marriage as two patterns of life that Christians believe exemplify the call to self-denial and self-discipline. The chapter finishes by asking what sex is for, and what kinds of self-discipline or self-denial are called for in sexual relationships. The chapter declares that disagreements between Christians 'in relation to the patterns of discipline appropriate for lesbian and gay people' are not 'disagreements about whether Christians are called to self-denial and restraint. They are disagreements about the specific disciplines we are called to and about

---

[19] *Living in Love and Faith*, p. 217.

the ways in which those disciplines work for people in different situations.'[20]

Part Four – Seeking answers: how do we hear God?
The purpose of this part (Chapters 13–18) is:

> to consider how we go about seeking and finding answers to the question, what does it mean for us as individuals and as a church to be Christlike when it comes to matters of identity, sexuality, relationships and marriage? And how is it that we reach different conclusions from one another about these things when we are all seeking to follow Jesus?[21]

Chapter 13: The Bible considers the unity and authority of the Bible, how the Bible should be read (both in general, and in relation to the biblical texts that have traditionally been seen as prohibiting same-sex relationships), different ways of understanding what the Bible tells us about marriage, and what Paul has to say about handling disagreement in the Church in Romans. The conclusion drawn by the chapter is that there are 'multiple forms of disagreement' about the Bible, which involve both disagreement about how to understand the biblical texts in their historical context and disagreement about the nature of biblical authority.[22]

Chapter 14: Church is in two main parts. The first part ('Listening to the tradition') looks at various forms of the church's tradition that are recognised as carrying authority and that shape our reading of the Bible: the rule of faith, the Creeds, the *Book of Common Prayer* and the Articles of Religion. It also looks at the church's role in the formation of the biblical canon and the role of bishops in upholding the church's tradition. The second part ('Listening to and as the whole body') looks at the whole church, national and worldwide, and its need to take counsel together to discern the will of God, looking at Acts 15 as a paradigmatic example of this.

---

[20] *Living in Love and Faith*, p. 258.
[21] *Living in Love and Faith*, p. 268.
[22] *Living in Love and Faith*, p. 308.

Chapter 15: Creation begins by noting that God speaks to us through the created world, but that the created world has been distorted by sin. It goes on to say that we need to listen to science in order to learn more about the world that God has made and to look at the arguments put forward for affirming the theological importance of natural knowledge as well as those put forward for questioning it.

Chapter 16: Cultural Context is concerned with Christian engagement with the surrounding culture. It declares that:

> Listening to the voice of God involves an ongoing process of discernment, in which we learn to recognize what in the Church and what in the wider world resonates with God's Word spoken in Jesus, and what muffles and distorts it.[23]

It argues that:

> There is no alternative but to listen hard to the people all around us, and to read and reread the sources of Christian faith in the light of the questions they ask, the criticisms they make, and the possibilities they present.[24]

As an example of Christian engagement with culture, the chapter looks at the development of Anglican thinking with regard to polygamy in Africa.

Chapter 17: Experience and conscience considers how our understanding of who we are and God's will for us is shaped by our experiences, our convictions and our experiences. It argues that we are all shaped by our experiences in regard to 'the questions we think most important, the methods we think most appropriate, the places we look for understanding, and so on'.[25] It goes on to say that we need to subject our convictions to processes of testing and discernment, and that, as Paul argues in 1 Corinthians 8:7–12, we need to 'take care with each other's consciences'.[26] Finally, the chapter cautions against either over- or under-

---

[23] *Living in Love and Faith*, p. 351.
[24] *Living in Love and Faith*, pp. 351–2.
[25] *Living in Love and Faith*, p. 354.
[26] *Living in Love and Faith*, p. 358.

estimating the importance of people's accounts of their 'convictions about their identities and relationships'.[27]

Chapter 18: Prayer and guidance looks in turn at dependence on prayer in the process of discernment in which we are engaged, at guidance as a spiritual gift, and the relation between prayer and the exercise of reason.

Part Five – Conversing: What can we learn from each other?
The purpose of this part is to invite the readers of the book, 'into a conversation between some of the people who have been involved in writing this book'.[28] This part consists of five 'scenes', each of which is 'based on a live conversation that was recorded, transcribed and edited' and each of which answers a different set of questions, as follows:[29]

Scene 1: A conversation about marriage – 'is marriage only between one man and one woman? Are there other forms of covenant that might be possible for other kinds of faithful committed relationships? Or should the nature of the Church of England's understanding of marriage be adapted to include same-sex couples?'

Scene 2: A conversation about sex and relationships – 'What boundaries should we place around sexual activity? Is its only proper place within marriage? Or are there other relationships which can find sexual expression?'

Scene 3: A conversation about gender identity and transition – 'Is our identity entirely God-given and to be accepted? Or do we play a part in making adjustments that help us to live into the identity we believe we are called to have?'

Scene 4: A conversation about the life of the Church – 'How do we respond to Jesus' call for unity in the light of difference and disagreement? How do we hold together holiness and love?'

An Appeal
As we have noted above, the bishops declare in their closing appeal that, in the face of the continuing disagreements among the bishops and in the Church as whole about the matters covered in the LLF material:

---

[27] *Living in Love and Faith*, p. 361.
[28] *Living in Love and Faith*, p. 378.
[29] *Living in Love and Faith*, p. 378.

all of us – bishops included – need to go on learning from each other and from all who seek the way of truth. That is the purpose of the Living in Love and Faith learning resources – to help us to learn and discern together so that right judgements and godly decisions can be made about our common life.[30]

The bishops go on to declare that their hope is that:

the Holy Spirit will use these learning resources to open a way for us to find our deepest convictions about Jesus Christ also affirmed by those who we presently disagree with.[31]

The bishops confess that they feel a tension 'between uniting the church in its differences and pressing for decisive decisions in the contested areas about which each of us feels strongly.'[32] However, they are united 'in our commitment to promote peace in the Church and to strive for the visible unity of the church.'[33]

7. What are we to make of the LLF book?

The positive teaching in the LLF *book*
First, the LLF book is clear about who God is. He is the God who is Father, Son and Holy Spirit and who became incarnate as Jesus Christ. Furthermore, the traditional Christian teaching about God's purposes and activity in creation and redemption are set out very clearly. For example, in the introduction to the Part Three, we are told that 'Christians are people who seek to live within, and become defined by' a particular story:[34]

It is a story that begins with God, who in love created humankind in the divine image, so that in communion with one another and with Christ we might mirror God's glory. It is a story about our

---

[30] *Living in Love and Faith*, p. 422.
[31] *Living in Love and Faith*, p. 422.
[32] *Living in Love and Faith*, p. 423.
[33] *Living in Love and Faith*, p. 423.
[34] *Living in Love and Faith*, p. 165.

rebellion, disobedience and refusal to depend on one another and on God – a disorder which has infected the whole of creation. It is a story of our desperate need for the mercy and love of God in the face of this sinfulness. It is a story about Jesus, who embraced our humanity, lived among us, and gave himself to death for us so that we and the whole of creation could be set free from the bonds of sin, the forces of evil and the judgement we deserve. It is a story of forgiveness, which invites us to repent daily and to reflect the love of God by forgiving others with the same measure with which we have been forgiven by God. It is the story of Jesus rising from the dead and ascending into heaven and interceding for us and for the whole creation. It is the story of the Church – his body on earth – inaugurated by the pouring out of the Holy Spirit among us so that we could experience the power of God's transforming love in our human weakness. It is a story about the end of death and the beginning of eternal life here and now. It is a story of faith in Jesus Christ, of hope in a new heaven and a new earth, and of the transforming power of God's love.[35]

Secondly, LLF is clear about the need for Christians individually and collectively to live a distinctive way of life that reflects the holiness of God who has created and redeemed them. Thus, in Chapter 12, we are told that the Christian community:

> is called to live a life together that has a definite character. That is why it requires discipline. This community is called to live a life that echoes and communicates God's holiness. They are called to shine with God's grace, mercy and love. They are called to be obedient together to the demands of this life. And, if they follow this calling, their life together will be

---

[35] *Living in Love and Faith*, p. 165.

distinctive. They will not live as those around them live.[36]

Thirdly, LLF includes a clear re-statement of the orthodox Christian understanding of marriage in Chapter 3: The gift of marriage. The Christian understanding of marriage is correctly grounded in the action of God at creation and quotes the words of Jesus:

> Have you not read that the one who made them at the beginning 'made them male and female', and said, 'For this reason a man shall leave his father and mother and be joined to his wife, and the two shall become one flesh'? So they are no longer two but one flesh. Therefore what God has joined together, let no one separate. (Matthew 19:4–6)[37]

It then comments:

> This is why the church's liturgy describes marriage as 'a gift of God in creation'. It is a gift given to bring life and to give life. God wants us to live fully and offers us ways to live that draw on God's life of love. The joining of a man and woman in marriage is a gift given together with the gift of humanity itself. It is a gift given 'at the beginning' – before God's people Israel were formed, before the law arrived and even before sin came. It is a gift given to all peoples.[38]

On the form of the marriage relationship, the chapter declares:

> Marriage's form, as described by Jesus, is the union of a man and a woman, and one that is intended to last for life. That is why the church's 'canons' (its laws), echoing the liturgies which have been heard in our land for centuries, say that 'Marriage is in its nature a union permanent and lifelong, for better for worse, till

---

[36] *Living in Love and Faith*, p. 221.
[37] *Living in Love and Faith*, p. 25.
[38] *Living in Love and Faith*, p. 25.

death them do part, of one man with one woman, to the exclusion of all others on either side'.[39]

The chapter also notes that in the Bible marriage is used as an image of 'Christ's union with the Church, and the final consummation of God's purpose for humanity'[40] and states that:

> God's good gifts of sexual desire and intimacy, with all their power and potential for good and harm, find their proper place and freest space in marriage. Here, the 'natural instincts and affections' that God has planted within us are 'hallowed' and to be 'rightly directed' for the purposes of love.[41]

The problems with the LLF book

These three positive elements of what is said in the LLF book need to be acknowledged. However, what also has to be acknowledged is that there are a lot of other elements in the material that are much less positive.

a) The book fails to give a proper account of the contemporary world and contemporary science

First, the account of contemporary British society and the place of religious faith within it (in Chapters 5 and 7) fail to address, or even acknowledge, the key issue of idolatry.

The information about the state of British society in Chapter 5 is factually correct. However, the chapter fails to reflect on the fact that behind the social trends that it notes lies an all-pervasive reality – that Britain has become a society that has increasingly turned its back on God and has turned instead to the twin idols of self-determination and the search for sexual fulfilment. These developments were charted by Carl Trueman in his important study, The Rise and Triumph of the Modern Self.[42] The chapter also fails to notice that the sexual revolution that has been the fruit of this idolatry has been deeply harmful in its effects. In the words of Glynn Harrison:

---

[39] *Living in Love and Faith*, p. 25.
[40] *Living in Love and Faith*, p. 32.
[41] *Living in Love and Faith*, p. 33.
[42] Carl Trueman, *The Rise and Triumph of the Modern Self* (Wheaton: Crossway, 2020).

en we stand back and survey the entire landscape of revolution, we witness injustice heaped upon lren, more people than ever living alone, the collapse of marriage among the poor, fatherless wastelands of social deprivation, and the pornographication of childhood.[43]

As Harrison goes on to say, what the sexual revolution gives us is, in fact, an object lesson in the futility of idolatry:

> One of the core messages of the gospel is that idols always ask for more and more, but give less and less until in the end they have everything and you have nothing. And so it is here. The irony is that after the revolution, even as they continue to obsess over their identities, people are not even having more or better sex than before. The core ideas of the revolution – 'be yourself,' 'find the you within you' – appear to be just another idolatry.[44]

LLF fails to note either of these points.

What LLF Chapter 7 says about current developments in religion is also factually correct, but again there is no analysis of what lies behind the developments to which it refers. It fails to acknowledge that these developments reflect the way that the secular Western idolatries of self-determination and sexual fulfilment are being actively promoted around the world. It also fails to recognise that changing attitudes towards human identity, sexuality and marriage both in Christianity and in other religions as well are a reflection of this. As is well known, we live in an increasingly interconnected and globalised world – and Western liberal idolatry is increasingly shaping this world.[45] This is a point that LLF totally overlooks.

Turning to what LLF says about science in Chapter 6, the one-sided emphasis the chapter places on the biological origins of same-sex attraction and confusion about sexual identity fails to do justice to the

---

43 Glynn Harrison, *A Better Story* (London: IVP, 2016), Kindle edition, loc. 1654.
44 Harrison, loc. 1654–1665.
45 For this point, see Gabrielle Kuby, *The Global Sexual Revolution* (Briar Noll: Angelico Press, 2015).

strong criticisms that have been made of the various theories of biological causation that have been put forward, and the strength of the evidence for social and psychological influences instead.[46]

The chapter also fails to acknowledge that the extreme variety of forms of same-sex attraction and transgender that exist today, and that have existed historically, mean that that causation is probably best seen in very specific terms particular to each individual. A one-size explanation definitely will not fit all. In addition, the discussion in Chapter 6 fails to note that causal influences do not negate free will and individual responsibility. Whatever the influences upon them, in the last instance, people choose whether to engage in same-sex sexual activity, to identify as transgender, and to go through gender transition.[47]

Chapter 6 also fails to note that serious flaws have been identified in the study which it cites to show that the effects of gender transition are beneficial[48] and conversely fails to take seriously the studies that call into question whether gender transition procedures are beneficial at all.[49] In addition, the dismissal in this chapter of 'sexual orientation and gender identity change efforts' ignores: the evidence that such efforts are found beneficial by a good number of people; the fact there is no convincing evidence that change therapy is always and necessarily harmful; and the moral issue of it being wrong to stop people having freedom to seek

---

[46] For an overview, see Neil and Briar Whitehead, *My Genes Made Me Do It! Homosexuality and the Scientific Evidence* (Whitehead Associates, 2020), J Alan Branch, *Born This Way?: Homosexuality, Science, and the Scriptures* (Bellingham: Lexham Press 2016).

[47] For these points see Mark Yarhouse, *Understanding Gender Dysphoria* (Downers Grove: IVP Academic, 2015); Branch, *Born This Way?*

[48] For these criticisms, see Nathaniel Blake, 'What We Don't Know: Does Gender Transition Improve the Lives of People with Gender Dysphoria?' *The Public Discourse*, 30 April 2019 at https://www.thepublicdiscourse.com/2019/04/51524/

[49] See, for example, Ryan Anderson, *When Harry Became Sally* (New York: Encounter Books, 2018), Ch. 5, and Ryan Anderson '"Transitioning" Procedures Don't Help Mental Health, Largest Dataset Shows', *The Heritage Foundation*, 3 August 2020 at https://www.heritage.org/gender/commentary/transitioning-procedures-dont-help-mental-health-largest-dataset-shows.

assistance to change or manage their feelings and desires, if that is what they desire to do.[50]

More generally the chapter does not acknowledge that even without specific change efforts people's sexual attraction is often fluid, changing over the course of their life for a whole variety of reasons. This means that the idea that the world can be neatly divided into those who are 'gay' and those who are 'straight', or 'homosexual' and 'heterosexual' is a big mistake. The world is a lot more complicated than that.[51]

Lastly, the chapter fails to acknowledge that the attribution of the mental (and physical) health issues faced by LGBTQI+ people to 'minority stress' has been challenged on the grounds that if this were the case, one would expect a reduction of these lesbian issues in more LGBTQI+ accepting societies, while this is not the case.[52]

What all this means is: while the LLF book is right to say that Christian engagement with the modern world needs to involve engagement with the findings of science, what it says about the findings of science is one-sided and misleading. As such, it does not provide a helpful contribution to Christian thinking about the causes of people's feelings of sexual attraction and sexual identity and the best way to respond to these.

b) The book fails to properly acknowledge what we learn from creation

Chapter 15: Creation rightly highlights the importance of paying attention to what we learn from creation when thinking about what it means to be human and to live rightly before God as human beings. However, the fundamental truth that the study of creation tells us is not taken sufficiently seriously: namely that, like other species of animals which God has created, humanity is a fundamentally dimorphic species

---

[50] See, for example, Belinda Brown, 'The Unscientific Roots of Bans on Conversion Therapy', *Mercator Net*, 11 November 2020 at https://mercatornet.com/unscientific-roots-of-conversion-therapy-ban/68137/ and the material on the website of the Core Issues Trust at https://www.core-issues.org/

[51] See Jenelle Williams Paris, *The End of Sexual Identity* (Downers Grove: Inter-Varsity Pres, 2011).

[52] See for example J Michael Bailey, 'The Minority Stress Model Deserves Reconsideration, Not Just Extension,' *Archives of Sexual Behavior*, vol. 49, pp. 2265–2268(2020).

– divided biologically and psychologically into males and females. From this we can deduce two important principles:

- Being male or female is not a choice, or a feeling, but a biological reality that cannot be changed even when people undergo gender transition procedures.

- Male and female human beings are biologically designed to have sexual intercourse with members of the other sex and to beget children as a result.[53]

The existence of people with intersex conditions does not challenge this basic truth for two reasons:

- The vast majority of intersex conditions do not call into question whether someone is male or female

- Even in the tiny percentage of people in whom elements of both sexes are present (and whose sex is therefore genuinely ambiguous) do not constitute a third type of human being. They are instead people in whom some form of developmental 'disorder' has occurred which has prevented them from developing as male and female in the normal way intended by God for his human creatures. The reason for saying that a 'disorder' has occurred is because the physical characteristics that make people intersex have no good purpose of their own and typically prevent the good ends that human sexual differentiation is meant to achieve – namely sexual intercourse and sexual reproduction.

All this is relevant to the key questions being addressed in LLF as to what it means to be human and to live rightly before God as a human being. For, as even the existence of intersex people testifies, God has created human beings as male and female. So, in order to respect and honour God's creative activity, we are called to live as members of the sex we have been created to be. It is not our role to attempt a new work of creation. Our role is to receive what we have been graciously given and to grow to

---

[53] For the evidence for this point, see Debra Soh, *The End of Gender: Debunking the Myths about Sex and Identity in Our Society* (New York: Threshold Editions, 2020).

maturity within the framework of what God has given. As Oliver O'Donovan states well:

> The sex into which we have been born (assuming it is physiologically unambiguous) is given to us to be welcomed as the gift of God. The task of psychological maturity – for it is a moral task, and not merely an event which may or may not transpire – involves accepting this gift and learning to love it, even though we may have to acknowledge that it does not come to us without problems. Our task is to discern the possibilities for personal relationship which are given to us with this biological sex, and to seek to develop them in accordance with our individual vocations. Those for whom this task has been comparatively unproblematic (though I suppose that no human being alive has been without some sexual problems) are in no position to pronounce any judgement on those for whom accepting their sex has been so difficult that they have fled from it into denial. Nevertheless, we cannot and must not conceive of physical sexuality as a mere raw material with which we can construct a form of psychosexual self-expression which is determined only by the free impulse of our spirits. Responsibility in sexual development implies a responsibility to nature – to the ordered good of the bodily form which we have been given.[54]

If so, seeking to live as a member of the opposite sex to our own, or seeking to adopt some other form of alternative sexual identity, is not only an attempt to achieve the impossible, since we cannot in fact escape the sex we were born into; it is also an act of rebellion against God our Creator. Our bodily form, and hence our sex, is a good given to us by God. As such, this is therefore something we are called on to accept rather than try to evade.

Secondly and similarly, having sex with someone of our own sex is likewise a rebellion against how we have been created. God has made us

---

[54] Oliver O'Donovan, *Begotten or Made?* (Oxford: OUP, 1984), pp. 28–29.

as creatures designed to have sex with the opposite sex. The very way we are made teaches us that to engage in same-sexual activity is to act in a way that is contrary to God's good will for his human creatures. For those who believe in the God who created nature, if something is 'contrary to nature', then it is contrary to God himself. Thus, although people may feel that it is right, their bodies are clearly telling them otherwise. This then explains what Paul is meaning when he says in Romans 1:26–27 that lesbian and gay sexual activity is 'against nature'.

These two basic deductions from creation are fundamental within a biblical worldview. Yet they are overlooked and never established within LLF, thus making it impossible for them to be built upon and then used in the contemporary Christian debate about human sexual identity and behaviour.

c) The book lacks clarity about the nature and authority of the Bible and about the overall biblical witness about human sexual identity and behaviour

Chapter 13 of the LLF book reminds its readers what Anglicans have traditionally believed about the Bible:

> Anglicans believe that the Bible is, in a classic phrase, 'God's Word written', and that God works through our reading of it. We believe these humans' words are words inspired by God (2 Timothy 3.16) and that we can hear God speak to us through them.[55]

Unfortunately, the chapter then undercuts this clear affirmation by setting out seven different views of the nature and authority of the Bible. It sets out the various views involved in a very fair way, but it does not reach any overall conclusion, leaving the reader with the impression that any of the approaches mentioned might be acceptable.

What it fails to note is that, in the end, only the first three approaches it outlines are compatible with historic position of the Christian church, rooted in the teaching of Jesus' himself.[56] It also fails to note that the Bible, both as a whole and in all its parts, gives us a clear, consistent and

---

[55] *Living in Love and Faith*, p. 275.
[56] See John Wenham, *Christ and the Bible* (Downers Grove: Intervarsity Press, 1973).

authoritative message from God about what we should believe and how we should live.

In addition, the LLF book does not acknowledge that the Bible give us a clear account of human sexual identity and how God wants his creatures to live. What we learn from the Bible, as we learn the created order, is that God has created two sexes, male and female, and has given sexual intercourse as the means by which they are to 'be fruitful and multiply (Genesis 1:28). What we also learn from the Bible – that goes beyond what we learn from creation – is that God has created marriage between one man and a woman as the sole God-given setting for sexual intercourse and the begetting and raising of children (Genesis 2:18–25).

These two truths then form the basis of what is said in the Bible as whole about human sexual identity and behaviour. The Bible sees human beings as males or females and prohibits any attempt to behave as thought this were not the case (see Deuteronomy 22:5 and 1 Corinthians 11:2–16) and consistently teaches, both explicitly and implicitly, that all forms of sexual activity outside marriage are contrary to God's will and off limits to God's people. (This is why the New Testament forbids porneia, that is, all forms of sexual activity outside heterosexual marriage).

Chapter 13 of the LLF book looks at seven texts concerning same-sex sexual relationships – Genesis 19, Judges 19, Leviticus 18:22 and 20:13, Romans 1:26–27, 1 Corinthians 6:9–11, and 1 Timothy 1:8–11. These texts are, contrary to what is suggested in the chapter, clear in their prohibition of all forms of same-sex sexual activity and not just some forms of it, and do not 'open the possibility of approving faithful, committed same sex relationships'.[57] They are not outliers that can be separated from the message of the Bible as a whole. On the contrary, they are the consistent outworking of the Biblical belief that God has created the world and humanity in a certain way and that he calls his people under both the Old and New Covenants to live in accordance with this fact and to abstain from forms of behaviour that are not in accordance with it.

---

[57] See Michael Brown, *Can You Be Gay and Christian?* (Lake Mary: Front line, 2014), Richard Davidson, Flame of Yahweh – Sexuality in the Old Testament (Peabody: Hendrickson, 2007), Chapter 4; Martin Davie, *Studies in the Bible and same-sex relationships since 2003* (Malton: Gilead Books 2013); Robert Gagnon, *The Bible and Homosexual Practice* (Nashville: Abingdon Press, 2001); and Ian Paul, *Same- sex Unions: The Key Biblical Texts* (Cambridge: Grove Books, 2014).

All these points are clear in the Bible, and they have been consistently affirmed by the Christian church in all its various branches for the whole of Christian history up until the last sixty years.[58] However, as in the case of the witness of creation, the LLF book lacks clarity when it comes to applying them to the modern Christian debate about human sexual identity and behaviour.

d) The LLF book fails to take proper account of the teaching of Jesus

While Chapter 12 of the LLF book does look at Jesus' teaching on sexual ethics, it fails to note that:

- Jesus roots his sexual ethics in God's creation of human beings as male and female and his joining them together in marriage

- Jesus did not reject the teaching of the Old Testament law on sexual ethics but rather intensified it by including desire as well action (Matthew 5:27–30) and by taking stricter line on divorce (Matthew 19:3–12)

- Jesus' condemnation of porneia (Mark 7:14–23) would have included a condemnation of same-sex sexual activity within its scope which means that we have to conclude that, like other Jews of the second Temple period, Jesus regarded same-sex relationships (of whatever type) as contrary to the will of God.[59] Any other view of the matter does not do justice to the historical evidence.[60]

---

[58] See S Donald Fortson III and Rollin Grams, *Unchanging Witness: The consistent Christian teaching on homosexuality in Scripture and Tradition* (Nashville: B&H Academic, 2016).

[59] The Jewish people of his day were remarkable in the ancient world for their consistent stance in opposition to same-sex sexual activity. This was one of the key aspects of Hellenistic life which they had fiercely resisted unto death at the time of the Maccabean revolt in 167 BC. The evidently saw this as a key distinctive hallmark of what it meant to be the redeemed people of the Creator God, displaying to the Gentiles how their God wanted human beings to live. Jesus did not imply that he thought they had over-reacted. Instead all the evidence indicates that he stood four-square with them in this view of the matter.

[60] For these points see, for example, Gagnon, Ch. 3, and John Nolland, 'Sexual Ethics and the Jesus of the Gospels,' *Anvil*, vol. 26 no. 1 (2009). It is also worth noting the point made by Andy Angel in his book *Intimate Jesus* (London: SPCK, 2017, Ch. 4) that John deliberately uses language with homoerotic overtones in

It also fails to explore what it means for our view of sexual ethics if that was the view taken by God incarnate. Can we be Christians and disagree with what Jesus thought about same-sex relationships?

Jesus welcomed the outsider and the outcast, including those rejected by his society because of their sexual misbehaviour. However, it is impossible to separate Jesus' call to follow him and his welcome of sinners from a call to repentance and discipleship (see Matthew 16:24–25, Mark 1:15, Luke 5:32, 19:1–10). If we ask what repentance and discipleship involved then, this leads us back to Jesus' rigorous sexual ethic described above.[61] The LLF book completely fails to explore this.

What LLF doesn't ask is this: if Jesus required from his first disciples an obedience to his sexual ethic that involved a rejection of same-sex relationships, on what basis might it be suggested that this requirement does not apply to the church today? How can the church take a different approach from her Lord?

And, for those of us who confess the Nicene Creed, the stance of the historical Jesus on this matter is simultaneously the stance of God incarnate. How can people confess Jesus as God incarnate and yet beg to disagree with his sexual ethic?

e) The LLF book does not acknowledge the need to evaluate experience, conscientious conviction and culture in the light of the witness of creation and the Bible

Chapter 17 of the LLF book is right to say that our beliefs will be shaped by our experiences. However, what it does not do is address the question of how we determine when our experiences have led us to believe things that are true and when they have led us to believe things that are false.

What it fails to say is that we need to be as self-aware as possible, thinking critically, about our experiences through the use of reason which is informed by God's revelation of himself in creation and the Bible and assisted by the voices of other Christians as reflected in the Christian

---

his account of the Last Supper in John 13 in order to make the point that the Greek ideal of an intimate relationship between men finds its fulfilment not in homosexual activity but in sharing in the eternal love between Jesus and his heavenly Father.

[61] For the rigorous implication of discipleship in the teaching of Jesus see Andy Angel, *The Jesus You Really Didn't Know* (Eugene: Wipf and Stock, 2019).

theological tradition. This is, at an individual level, an outworking of the classic Anglican methodology of discerning God's will for the church through the witness of Scripture, Tradition and Reason.

In the relation to the debate about human sexual identity and behaviour, this means reviewing our experiences in the light of the truth of how God created his human creatures as male and female and ordained marriage as the setting for sexual intercourse, procreation and the raising of children. The point the book should have made is that we need to reinterpret our experiences in the light of this truth.

What the book should also have done is invite its readers to think critically about the accounts of people's experiences given in the 'Encounters' sections of the book. It is right that the book draws attention to what people have to say about their experiences – because engaging with other people in relation to questions of human sexual identity and behaviour needs to involve listening to their experiences so that we understand the personal basis on which they approach these issues. However, what it does not mean is that we should accept what they have to say about their experiences as 'gospel'. Just as we can interpret our own experiences wrongly, so can other people and we need to have the intellectual tools to critically evaluate what they tell us. The LLF book does not provide such tools.

In addition, while due regard has to be given to people's conscientious convictions (as the church has accepted ever since Paul wrote on this topic in Roman 14:1–23 and 1 Corinthians 8:1–13, 10:23–33), LLF Chapter 17 fails to note that such convictions cannot be legitimate grounds for doing things that are objectively wrong. A terrorist may have a profound conscientious conviction of the rightness of their cause, but if they kill without legitimate authority, their action is still, nonetheless, murder. Similarly, someone may be profoundly convinced that they are meant to be in a relationship with someone who is married to someone else, but their action would nonetheless be adultery and therefore wrong. One can multiply such examples almost indefinitely, and what it means for the issues addressed by LLF is this: the fact that people believe that is right to be in a same-sex relationship or be transgender does not mean that this is the case, or that the church should make accommodation for their convictions.

The LLF book should have made this point and then discussed why the witness of creation and the Bible mean that that the church should not accept people's convictions that they should be in same-sex sexual relationships, or should identify as transgender.

Chapter 16 of the LLF book is right when it says that Christians need to engage with surrounding culture, and it is also right when it warns that this a complex process. However, in the end, the chapter really just ends up saying, 'it's all very difficult' – rather than providing any theological principles to guide such engagement. What it should have done is explore how Christians should understand and engage with culture using the twin witness of nature and the Bible as their starting point, and then applied this approach in relation to the matters being discussed in LLF, highlighting the point made earlier in this paper that the sexual permissiveness of our culture is the outworking of a turning from God to idolatry and, as such, something that Christians should challenge rather than accept or adopt.

It should also be noted that what is said about the developing Anglican approach to polygamy in Chapter 16 is correct as far as it goes. However, it fails to make the critical point that this development did not involve any fundamental change in Christian ethics or the church's understanding and practice of marriage. All it did was to ask how best to apply Christian teaching in way that did not have the unintended consequence of harming vulnerable people — women and children now abandoned by their husbands and fathers and left destitute. What needs to be highlighted, and what LLF fails to highlight, is that there is thus no analogy between this development and the acceptance of same-sex relationships or the introduction of same-sex marriages since the latter would involve a fundamental change in Christian sexual ethics and in the church's understanding and practice of marriage.

f) The LLF book wrongly leaves open the question of what constitutes appropriate Christian conduct.

This last point leads on to the next problem with the LLF book which is that fails to give answers to the issues which it raises. The book is correct when it says in Chapter 10 that there are 'deep disagreements' in the Church of England:

> about whether certain aspects of human experience, in
> the areas of gender and sexuality, are to be viewed as

reflecting the goodness and God-given diversity of humans as created in God's image, or as marks of the brokenness of that created image which God is working to restore.[62]

It is also correct when it says in Chapters 11 and 12 that the overarching question facing the Church of England is 'Which patterns of life are consistent, and which inconsistent, with God's holiness?' and that the current disagreements within it are disagreements about 'the specific disciplines' to which Christians are called and 'the ways in which those disciplines work for people in different situations.'[63]

The problem is that having made these points, the LLF book then fails to say how these issues should be resolved. What the book ought to have gone on to say is that:

- same-sex sexual attraction and difficulties with accepting one's given sexual identity are a result of creation's brokenness rather than its diversity

- engaging in same-sex sexual activity or adopting a transgender identity are inconsistent with the holiness to which God calls his people

- the basic disciplines to which all Christians are called are to live as the men and women God created them to be (avoiding porneia by abstaining from all forms of sexual activity outside marriage, including all forms of same-sex sexual activity) are particularly to be observed by those who are called by God to ordained or licensed lay ministry since ministers are called to be particularly exemplary in their way of life

By failing to make these points the LLF book contributes to the current confusion in the Church of England by giving the impression that different opinions on these matters may have equal validity.

g) The LLF book overlooks two crucial points when it talks about paying attention to the 'mind of the Church'

Chapter 14 of the LLF book is right when it says we need to pay attention to the 'mind of the Church'. It is made known to us through the Creeds

---

[62] *Living in Love and Faith*, p. 217.
[63] *Living in Love and Faith*, pp. 234 and 258.

and other documents from the history of the church that are accepted as theologically authoritative and we need to take counsel together to address difficult and divisive issues, as Christians have done from the earliest years of the church's existence.

However, it fails to acknowledge that the historic mind of the church is clear about the basics of human identity and sexual ethics. As noted above, it is only in the last sixty years that the church has begun to doubt that sex is only meant to take place within heterosexual marriage. The church's historic rule has been simple: sexual faithfulness within heterosexual marriage and sexual abstinence outside it. If due weight is to be given to Christian tradition, this fact needs to be taken into account and very good grounds would have to be given for saying we now know that this rule is wrong – grounds which the book fails to provide.

It also fails to acknowledge that the decisions of the councils of the church only carry weight if they are in agreement with Scripture and not otherwise. This means that the fact that Christians in the Church of England should only take note of the conciliar decisions of other churches on matters currently under discussion if it can be shown that these decisions are in line with what Scripture says. Thus, the decisions of the Episcopal Church or the Church of Sweden to allow same-sex marriages to be celebrated in their churches should carry no weight for the Church of England unless these decisions can be shown to be biblical. As Article XXI notes, councils 'may err, and sometimes have erred, even in things pertaining unto God' and biblical teaching is the measure for determining whether this has been the case.[64]

h) There are important issues which the LLF book fails to address, and it fails to give any advice on pastoral care

Although the LLF book covers a wide range of issues, there are still important issues relating to 'identity, sexuality, relationships and marriage' that are not discussed. Thus, there is no exploration of whether the Church of England's current disciplines with regard to contraception, divorce and re-marriage are theologically correct, and there is no discussion of the ethical issues relating to cohabitation, masturbation, pornography, prostitution, sex-surrogacy, and treatments for infertility. In addition, there is no discussion of what it might mean for those people

---

[64] Article XXI, *Thirty-Nine Articles*, 1571.

with intersex conditions whose sex is genuinely ambiguous to live rightly before God.

As was the case with the shared conversations which preceded it, the focus of the LLF book is on the issue of same-sex sexual relationships, with a limited amount of coverage of the issues of transgender and intersex. It is important to discuss these issues, but it is not acceptable is to ignore the other issues to do with 'identity, sexuality, relationships and marriage' that affect the lives of the large majority of people who are not same-sex attracted or transgender, as the LLF does,

In addition, the LLF book says nothing at all about the key issue of how to care pastorally for those who are struggling in the areas of identity, sexuality, relationships and marriage. What does appropriate pastoral care by clergy and congregations look like in these cases? That is something people really need to know – and the book gives no help at all in this regard.

i) The LLF book fails to give a proper account of the role of bishops in the life of the church and fails to give adequate episcopal guidance to the church

Chapter 14 of the LLF book quotes the words of the 1662 Ordinal which describe the role of the bishop as being to 'banish and drive away all erroneous and strange doctrine contrary to God's Word; and both privately and openly to call upon and encourage others to the same.'[65] It then goes on to say that this means that:

> Bishops will, collectively, look at how deeply the pattern of teaching in the church as a whole is sending down roots into the Bible, how richly it is informed by the Christian tradition, how attentive it is to what we know of the natural world, and how seriously participants in it are engaging with their mission context and with one another's deep convictions. They will look at how well the church is encouraging, resourcing, and making use of those who do have formal and informal teaching roles. They will make judgements about how present teaching relates to the limits that earlier generations of the church have

---

[65] *Living in Love and Faith*, p. 318.

identified as necessary to protect the overall health of the Christian faith.[66]

There are two problems with what is said in this quotation. First, it fails to make clear that the responsibility of the bishops to counter 'all erroneous and strange doctrine' is not only a collective, but also an individual one. Each individual bishop has a personal responsibility before God to do this regardless of what his or her fellow bishops do (or fail to do). Secondly, the quotation fails to make the basic point that bishops are called to take action to banish 'all erroneous and strange doctrine.' They have to clearly and publicly reject it themselves, and do all in their power to make sure it is not propagated and does not take root in that area of the Church of England for which they are responsible.

Not only does the LLF book thus fail to give a proper account of the role of the bishops, but the book itself is an example of the bishops failing to perform that role. For the reasons set out at the start of this paper, the call to 'banish and drive away all erroneous and strange doctrine' in regard to the issues under discussion in LLF means taking action to counter the acceptance of gender transition, same-sex marriages, same-sex sexual relationships and all other forms of sexual activity outside heterosexual marriage. In the LLF book, the bishops fail to take this action. Nowhere in the Foreword, or in the Appeal, or the Invitation, or in the rest of book (for which they are also ultimately responsible), do they say these things are wrong and that Christians should not think or teach otherwise, or act as if they were not wrong. This means that, in regard to LLF, the bishops have simply not properly fulfilled their episcopal responsibilities. They have not done what they are called to do.

8. What are we to make of the other LLF resources?

The LLF Course
The five-session LLF course is basically a summary introduction to the main ideas in the LLF book with questions for individual thought or group discussion. As such, its strengths and weaknesses mirror those of the book. It will help people to begin to understand what the current debate in the Church of England is about, but what it does not do is give its participants the information they need to make proper decisions about

---

[66] *Living in Love and Faith*, p. 319.

these matters. As with the book, the big problem is that it does not start in the right place and move out from there.

It does not acknowledge that the correct starting point for our thinking about identity, sex and marriage is the truth revealed in nature and Scripture; that all humans are created by God as part of a dimorphic species consisting of males and females; and that God ordained marriage between a man and woman as the proper setting for sexual intercourse and for the procreation of children and as sign of his relationship with his people in this world and in the world to come. It does not then acknowledge that this means that humans are called to live as the men and women God created them to be (as determined by their biology) and to either relate sexually to a member of the opposite sex in marriage or be sexually abstinent. The fallenness of the world means that we all struggle to live in the light of these truths in various ways, but this does not mean that we are free as individuals to reject these truths in the way we live, or that the church can say that people do not have to live by them.

Because it does not do these things the course fails to give a properly truthful perspective on the matters currently under debate. Like the book, the course also fails to recognise that there are a number of other very important issues concerning sex, relationships and marriage other than the two issues of same-sex relationships and transgender.

The podcasts and the films
The podcasts and films are good ways of understanding discussions that took place in LLF and that led to the LLF book, and the real-life stories that underly the current debate in the Church of England about matters to do with identity, sexuality, relationships and marriage. The problem is that, as with the LLF book, there are no tools provided to help people assess the various arguments offered in the podcasts, or to think theologically about the stories told in the films.

The LLF library
The same problem also exists with the hundreds of items available through, or listed in, the LLF library. People will need help to know what to read and to make sense of what they read and to think critically about it and to decide what is true and what is not, and LLF offers no help in this regard. No responsible college tutor would simply point their students to the college library and say, 'Go on then, make sense of that lot' – and yet that is effectively what LLF is doing with its library.

9. Conclusion

If we ask whether the LLF resources provide the guidance that Christians need to know how to maintain a faithful and distinctive Christian witness in today's society the answer, unfortunately is 'no.' As noted above, Christians in Britain live in a society which has increasingly turned from the worship of God to worshipping the idols of self-determination and the search for sexual fulfilment. In the face of this situation, Christians in this country need clear guidance on a range of matters:

- They need clear teaching about who the true God is and how we can know his will for his human creatures.

- They need clear teaching about the idolatrous nature of contemporary society and how its idolatrous nature is manifested in the way people behave.

- They need clear teaching about what to say to others about why idolatry and idolatrous behaviour are to be rejected and why a life based on worship and obedience of the one true God is to be embraced instead.

- They need clear teaching about how to live in a distinctive way themselves and how to show love and support to others who find living in this way difficult.

- They need clear teaching about the fact that living in a distinctive way involves living as the men and women they were created to be, and living lives of sexual holiness marked by a rejection of *porneia*.

The LLF resources give help with the first half of the first bullet point – and that is it. Those who want help with the rest will need to look elsewhere.

The big problem with the LLF material is that, in a desire not to be seen to be taking sides, it basically gives equal weight to all opinions (except in the area of science where it is distinctly one-sided). The effect of this is to move the Church of England to a more liberal position by implicitly suggesting that liberal ideas should be taken as seriously as those that reflect the church's traditional teaching. The fundamental failure of LLF is that it fails to acknowledge that there is a clear pattern of sexual identity and behaviour in Scripture, endorsed by Jesus himself, and supported by what nature teaches us, that is reflected in the church's traditional teaching and practice, but rejected by those who wish to change them (or, in the case of transgender, have changed them already).

The purpose of the LLF material is to give Christians in the Church of England the information they need to make informed decisions about the church's future. Because of the fundamental failure just mentioned, LLF the material fails to do this. Those in the Church of England who continue to accept orthodox Christian teaching and practice need to engage with the LLF material by acknowledging its strengths, explaining its weaknesses, and giving the clear Christian teaching about sexual identity and behaviour that LLF fails to provide so that the church is properly informed by the time there are votes in General Synod.

Recently Released by the Latimer Trust

What does the Bible really say? Addressing Revisionist Arguments on Sexuality and the Bible *by Martin Davie*

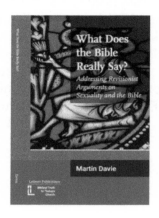

In 2019 a series of ten articles by various authors was published on the liberal Anglican website ViaMedia.News under the collective title 'Does the Bible Really Say....?' The purpose of this series was to challenge the belief that the Bible rules out acceptance of same-sex sexual relationships and same-sex marriage.

The essays in this book are response to these ViaMedia.News articles. They show that the arguments that these articles put forward are not sustainable in the light of what the Bible actually says. Underlying the current debate in the Church about human sexuality is the question asked of Eve by the snake 'Did God really say?' (Genesis 3:1). Through nature and Scripture God has said clearly that he has created human beings as male and female and has ordained marriage between one man and one woman as the sole legitimate setting for sexual intercourse. We know that this is what God has told us and yet in the face of pressure from our contemporary culture we are tempted to question whether this is what he really meant.

It is of the utmost importance that this temptation is resisted. The purpose of this book is to encourage such resistance.

A Basic Christian Primer on Sex, Marriage and Family Life, *by Martin Davie*

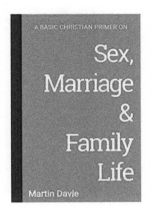

We live in an age in which there is widespread confusion about matters to do with sex, marriage, and family life not only in society at large, but also within the Christian Church.

The purpose of this new Primer is to address this confusion by providing clergy and laity alike with a basic introduction to what the Christian faith has to say about these matters. It is particularly designed to help Christians to understand the issues that will be discussed in the Church of England following the publication of the Living in Love and Faith material in late 2020.

The Primer explains in clear terms the basis of a Christian approach to these matters, and then goes on to look at what Christianity has to say about marriage, singleness, friendship, intersex and transgender, sex outside marriage (including same-sex relationships), divorce and re-marriage, birth control and treatment for infertility.

To Tell the Truth. *Basic questions and Best explanations.*
by J. Andrew Kirk

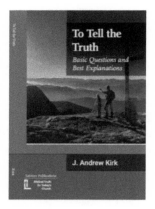

Human beings are inquisitive people. We all, quite rightly, like to explore the real world in its many fascinating dimensions. In particular, there are a few deep questions that most people face at some time in their lives: Who are we? Is there an overall purpose for our lives? What is good to believe? Why is there so much evil and suffering around? How is evil to be overcome and suffering accounted for? What best can help us to know how we should live? What is truth and how can we know it?

For well over a millennium and a half the Christian Faith has guided the Western world and, more recently, other parts of the world in how to answer these and many other questions. However, its answers have also been strongly disputed, sometimes with hostile intent. In this book, Andrew Kirk argues strongly that the Christian Faith, in spite of all that has been thrown against it, still represents by far and away the best explanations for these profound enigmas of life. Here you will find convincing answers, and reasons why alternative ideas do not ultimately match the full realities of our existence.

In our Anglican Foundations series

'Doubt not ... but Earnestly Believe' *A fresh look at the BCP Baptist Service.* by *Mark Pickles*

Whilst Common Worship (2000) provides a Book of Common Prayer Communion (BCP) in modern English, sadly there is no such provision for the BCP baptism service. For some Anglican evangelicals this may not seem to be a particularly regrettable omission.

There are those who might not be persuaded of the biblical mandate for baptising infants, whilst others might have concerns over some of the language used that may appear to affirm 'baptismal regeneration'. This booklet is an attempt not only to engage with those questions and concerns but also to proffer an enthusiastic support for the theology and liturgical content of the BCP Baptism service. It has a great emphasis on the covenantal grace of God which encourages Christian parents to "doubt not – but earnestly believe" in God's faithfulness and mercy. In so doing it directs our primary focus to our promise keeping God and not to ourselves.

Lightning Source UK Ltd.
Milton Keynes UK
UKHW010758260721
387780UK00003B/724